Audio Access Included

FRETBOARD ROADMAPS MANDOLIN

THE ESSENTIAL PATTERNS THAT ALL THE PROS KNOW AND USE

BY FRED SOKOLOW AND BOB APPLEBAUM

T0048542

To access audio visit:
www.halleonard.com/mylibrary

Enter Code
6898-3064-9639-0261

RECORDING CREDITS
Mandolin, Guitar, Banjo, and Vocals—Fred Sokolow
Sound Engineer and Other Instruments—Dennis O'Hanlon
Recorded at O'Hanlon Recording and Music Services

ISBN 978-0-634-00142-0

HAL•LEONARD®
7777 W. BLUEMOUND RD. P.O. BOX 13819 MILWAUKEE, WI 53213

Visit Hal Leonard Online at
www.halleonard.com

SONG INDEX

CONTENTS

INTRODUCTION

Accomplished mandolin players can *ad lib* hot solos and play backup in any key—all over the fretboard. They know several different soloing approaches and can choose the style that fits the tune, whether it's hard driving bluegrass, blues, rock, folk music or an Italian song.

There are moveable patterns on the mandolin fretboard that make it easy to do these things. The pros are aware of these "fretboard roadmaps," even if they don't read music. If you want to really know your instrument or jam with other players, *this is essential mandolin knowledge.*

You need the fretboard roadmaps if…

▶ All your soloing sounds the same and you want some different styles and flavors from which to choose.

▶ You don't know how to play in any key.

▶ Your mandolin fretboard beyond the 5th fret is mysterious, uncharted territory.

▶ You can't automatically play any familiar melody.

▶ You know a lot of "bits and pieces" on the mandolin, but you don't have a system that ties it all together.

Read on, and many mysteries will be explained. If you're serious about playing mandolin, the pages that follow can shed light and save you a great deal of time.

Good luck,

Fred Sokolow

THE RECORDING AND THE PRACTICE TRACKS

All the licks, riffs and tunes in this book are played on the accompanying recording. There are also four *Practice Tracks*. Each is in a different musical genre and offers an example of specific techniques, such as moveable major scales or chop chord licks.

The songs are mixed so that the mandolin is on one side of your stereo and the backup band is on the other. You can also tune out the mandolin track and use the backup tracks to practice playing solos.

FIRST POSITION CHORDS

Here are some basic mandolin chords. The numbers indicate the left-hand fingering. Practice the chords by strumming the following simple tunes. Use a pick, and strum a downstroke for each chord/letter name (D, G7) or slash (/).

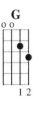     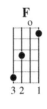

G **C** **D** **A** **E** **F** **Bb** *

   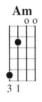

G7 **C7** **Dm** **Am** **Em** * **B7**

* The arc in the Bb and Em chords indicates a "barre." In barred chords, two or more strings are fretted by the same finger.

CAN THE CIRCLE BE UNBROKEN

     G / / /   C   /   G /
Can the circle be unbroken, bye and bye, Lord, bye and bye?

     G /   /   Em G   D   G /
There's a better home a-waiting, in the sky, Lord, in the sky.

RED RIVER VALLEY

     C   G7   C /   /   /   G7 /
Come and sit by my side if you love me. Do not hasten to bid me adieu.

   C   C7   F /   G7   /   C /
But remember the Red River Valley, and the cowboy who loved you so true.

AMAZING GRACE

E   /   A   E   /   /   B7 /
Amazing grace, how sweet the sound that saved a wretch like me.

E   /   A   E   /   B7 E /
I once was lost but now I'm found, was blind but now I see.

HOUSE OF THE RISING SUN

Dm F   G   Bb   Dm   F   A /
There is a house in New Orleans they call the Rising Sun.

    Dm   F   G   Bb   Dm A   Dm /
And it's been a the ruin of many a poor boy, and I, oh God, was one.

5

#1 NOTES ON THE FRETBOARD

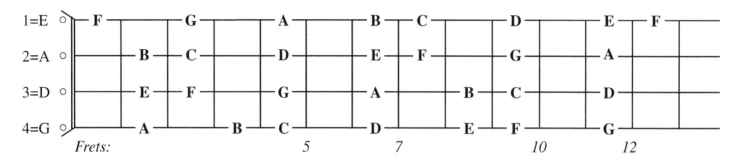

WHY?

▶ Knowing where the notes are will help you find chords and scales up and down the neck. It will help you alter and understand chords (e.g., *How do I flat the seventh in this chord? Why is this chord minor instead of major?*). It's a first step toward understanding music.

WHAT?

▶ *The notes get higher in pitch as you go up the alphabet and up the fretboard.*

▶ *A whole step is two frets, and a half step is one fret.*

▶ *Sharps are one fret higher:* 1st string/3rd fret = G, so 1st string/4th fret = G♯; 2nd string/5th fret = D, so 2nd string/6th fret = D♯.

▶ *Flats are one fret lower:* 1st string/5th fret = A, so 1st string/4th fret = A♭; 2nd string/2nd fret = B, so 2nd string/1st fret = B♭.

HOW?

▶ *Fretboard markings help.* Most mandolins have fretboard inlays on the neck at the 5th, 7th, 10th and 12th frets. Become aware of these signposts.

DO IT!

▶ *Starting with the 4th (lowest) string, the mandolin is tuned: G, D, A, E* (Great Danes Are Elegant). Memorize these notes!

▶ *These notes are repeated at the 12th fret:* the 1st (E) string at the 12th fret is E, the 2nd (A) string at the 12th fret is A, and so on.

▶ *When you fret a string at the 7th fret, it's the same note as the next-highest string.* The 4th string/7th fret is a D note, like the open (unfretted) 3rd string. The 3rd string/7th fret is A, like the open 2nd string. *This is a good way to check the mandolin's tuning.*

► *Learn other notes in reference to the notes you already know.*

▷ *The notes at the 5th fret are a whole step* (or one step of the alphabet) *lower than the 7th fret notes.* The 4th string/7th fret = D, so 4th string/5th fret = C.

▷ *The notes at the 10th fret are a whole step below the 12th fret notes.* The 3rd string/12th fret = D, so the 3rd string/10th fret = C.

▷ *Everything starts over at the 12th fret.* The 1st string/2nd fret (two frets above the open 1st string/E) is F♯, so the 1st string/14th fret (two frets above the 1st string/12th fret) is also F♯.

SUMMING UP — NOW YOU KNOW...

► *The location of the notes on the fretboard*

► *The meaning of these musical terms:*

Whole Step, Half Step, Sharp (♯), Flat (♭)

THE MAJOR SCALE

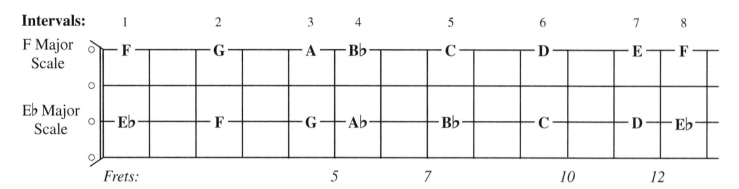

WHY?

▶ To understand music and to communicate with other players, you need to know about the major scale. The major scale is a ruler that helps you measure distances between notes and chords. Knowing the major scale will help you understand and talk about chord construction, scales and chord relationships. (The roadmaps here are for the purpose of seeing interval relationships, the roadmaps in the rest of the book contain mandolin-friendly scale diagrams.)

WHAT?

▶ *The major scale is the "Do-Re-Mi" scale you have heard all your life.* Countless familiar tunes are composed of notes from this scale.

▶ *Intervals are distances between notes.* The intervals of the major scale are used to describe these distances. For example, E is the third note of the C major scale, and it is four frets above C (see above). This distance is called a *third.* Similarly, A is a third above F, and C♯ is a third above A. On the mandolin, *a third is always a distance of four frets.*

HOW?

▶ *Every major scale has the same interval pattern of whole and half steps:*

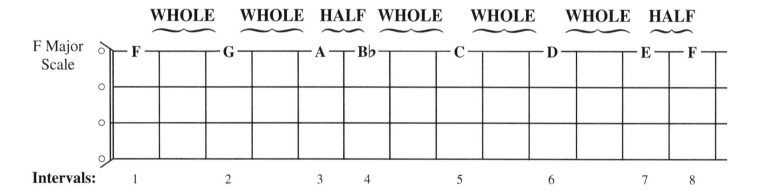

In other words, the major scale ascends by whole steps (two frets at a time) with two exceptions: there is a half step (one fret) from the third to the fourth notes and from the seventh to the eighth notes. It's helpful to think of intervals in terms of frets (e.g., a third is four frets).

► *Intervals can extend above the octave.* They correspond to lower intervals:

▷ A ***ninth*** is 2 frets above the octave. It's the same note as the ***second***, but an octave higher.

▷ An ***eleventh*** is 5 frets above the octave. It's the same note as the ***fourth***, but an octave higher.

F Major Scale

Intervals:

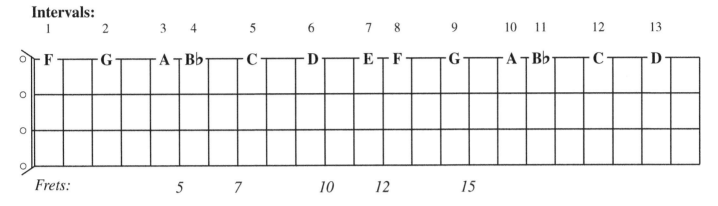

| 1 | 2 | 3 | 4 | 5 | 6 | 7 | 8 | 9 | 10 | 11 | 12 | 13 |

F G A Bb C D E F G A Bb C D

Frets: 5 7 10 12 15

DO IT!

► *Learn the major scale intervals* by playing any note and finding the note that is a third higher, a fourth and fifth higher, etc.

SUMMING UP — NOW YOU KNOW...

► *The intervals of the major scale and the number of frets that make up each interval*

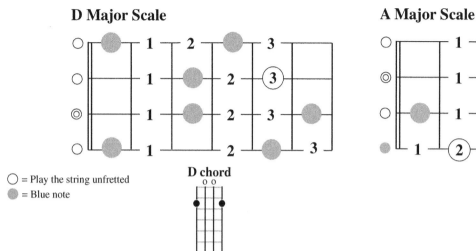

◆ #3 ◆ FIRST POSITION MAJOR SCALES: D AND A

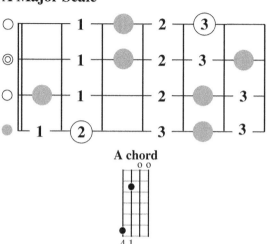

D Major Scale

A Major Scale

◯ = Play the string unfretted
⬤ = Blue note

D chord

A chord

WHY?

▶ Familiarity with these scales helps you play melodies and ad lib solos in the keys of A and D. These are the two easiest keys for mandolin because they include so many open strings. That's why so many fiddle tunes are in these keys; the violin is tuned the same as the mandolin.

WHAT?

▶ *Every key has its own scale and characteristic licks.* You use the D scale to play in the key of D, the A scale to play in A, and so on.

▶ *Each scale (and the licks that go with it) can be played throughout a tune,* in spite of chord changes within the tune.

▶ *A root is the note that gives the scale its name.* "D" is the root of the D major scale.

▶ *The root notes in each scale are circled.* The numbers are suggested fingerings.

▶ *The grey circles are "blue notes,"* flatted 3rds, 5ths and 7ths. They add a bluesy flavor to the scales.

HOW?

▶ *Put your hand "in position" for each scale by fingering the appropriate chord* (e.g., play a D chord to get in position for the D major scale). You don't have to maintain the chord while playing the scale, but it's a reference point.

▶ *Play "up and down" each scale (as written below) until it feels comfortable and familiar.* Play the chord before playing the scale, and "loop" the scale—play it several times in a row, with no pause between repetitions. Here are the two scales to practice:

D Major Scale

A Major Scale

DO IT!

► *Become familiar with the D and A major scales by playing the following scale exercises.*
Each can be played as written and backwards.

Ascending A Scale Exercise

Descending D Scale Exercise

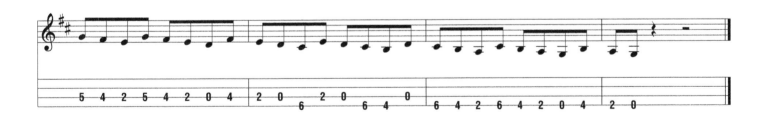

► "Nine Pound Hammer," is in the key of A. Both the verse and chorus are based on the A major scale, and the chorus emphasizes blue notes.

Nine Pound Hammer

► The next version of "Nine Pound Hammer" is just like the previous one, in the key of D.

Nine Pound Hammer (In D)

Here's the popular fiddle tune, "Arkansas Traveler," played in the key of D.

Arkansas Traveler

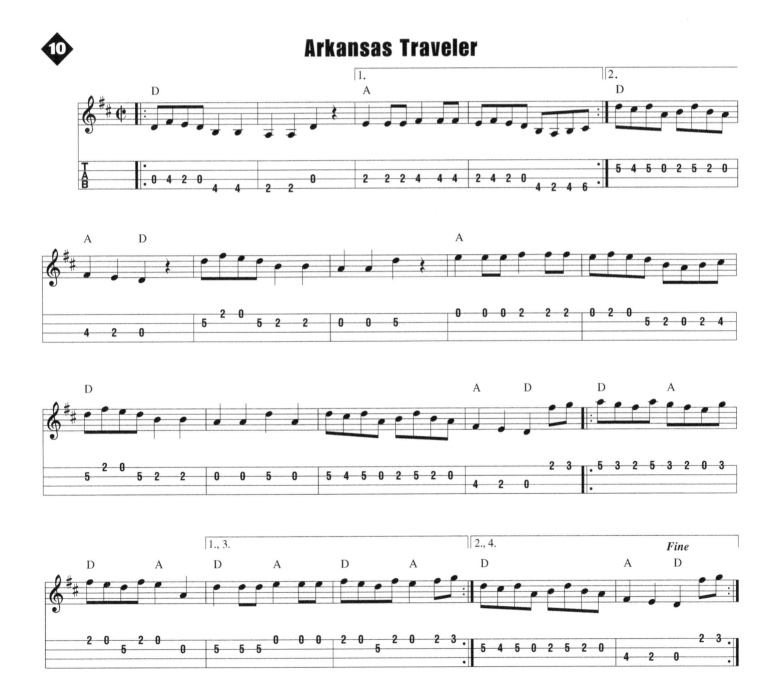

► *Double stops* (two harmonizing notes played simultaneously) **enrich your playing.** The first position A chord offers five double stops, and the first position D offers six:

First Position A Double Stops

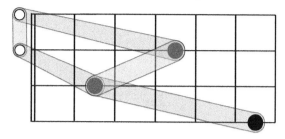 

First Position D Double Stops

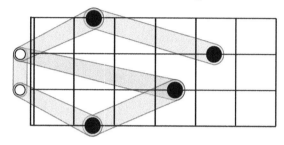 

The following version of an old two-chord folk song shows how to use the D and A double stops. This symbol 𝄎 indicates a *tremolo*, a very characteristic mandolin effect, produced by rapid up and down strokes. (Listen to Track 11.)

Down in the Valley

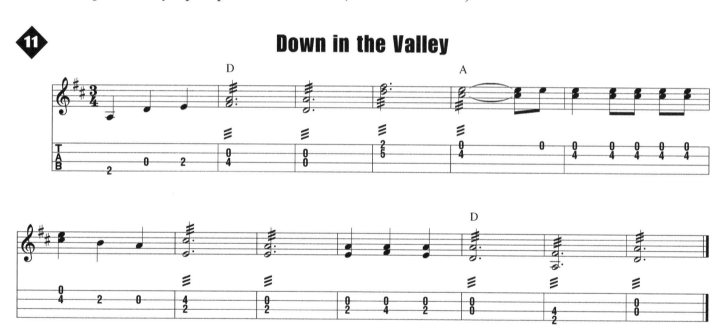

SUMMING UP — NOW YOU KNOW...

► *How to play two first-position major scales* (D and A) *and how to use them to play licks and solos*

► *The meaning of the musical term "blue notes," and how to add them to your major scales and licks*

► *How to play double stops for D and A chords*

► *The meaning of the term "root note"*

14

FIRST POSITION MAJOR SCALES: G AND C

G Major Scale

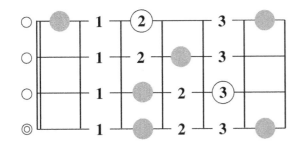

C Major Scale

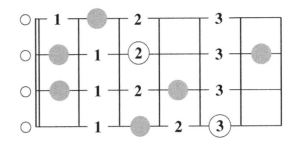

WHY?

► Once you're familiar with these two scales, it'll be easy to play melodies and solos in the keys of G and C.

WHAT?

► *The root notes in each scale are circled.* The numbers are suggested fingerings.

► *The grey circles are "blue notes,"* flatted 3rds, 5ths and 7ths.

HOW?

► *Put your hand "in position" for each scale by fingering the appropriate chord.*

► *Play each scale until it feels comfortable and familiar.*

G Major Scale

C Major Scale

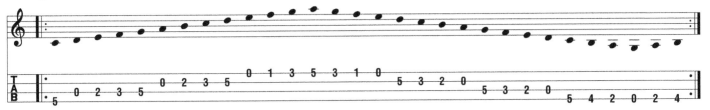

DO IT!

► *Become familiar with the G and C major scales by playing these scale exercises:*

Ascending G Scale Exercise

Descending C Scale Exercise

► The next tune shows how to use the G and C major scales to embellish a simple melody and ad lib solos. The old cowboy song, "Streets of Laredo," is played in the keys of G and C.

Streets of Laredo

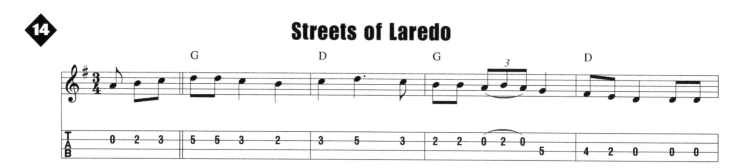

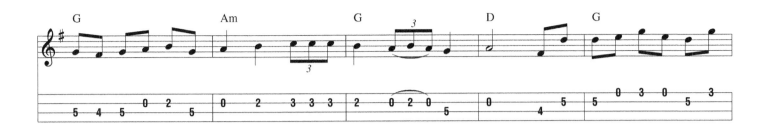
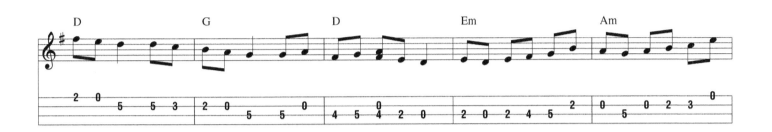

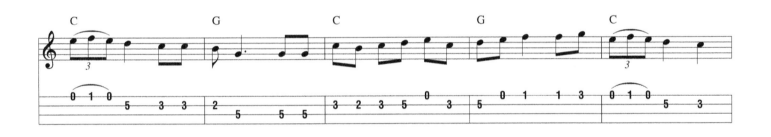
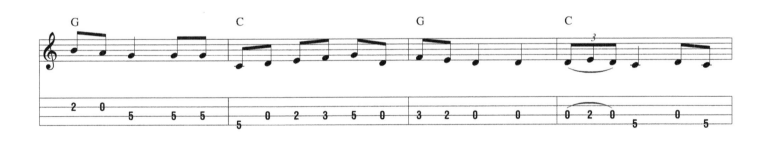

The following eight-bar blues is played twice in a row: first in G, then in C. The mandolin plays bluesy licks based on the G, then the C major scale.

Eight Bars and Eight Strings

▶ *You can use the major scale with blue notes to play songs in a minor key.* If you substitute the flatted third for the major third and occasionally play other blue notes (♭7ths and ♭5ths), the major scale becomes a minor scale. That's what the mandolin does in the Dixieland standard below, "Gambler's Blues," sometimes called "St. James Infirmary Blues."

Gambler's Blues

▶ *The following double stops can enrich your playing.* Use them as illustrated in the version of "Streets of Laredo" that follows.

First Position G Double-stops

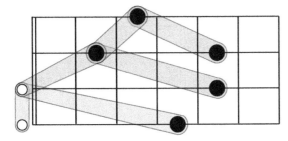

First Position C Double-stops

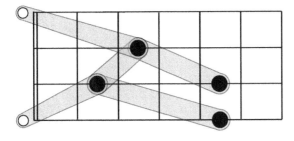

Streets of Laredo (With Double Stops)

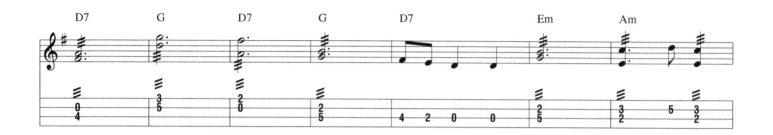

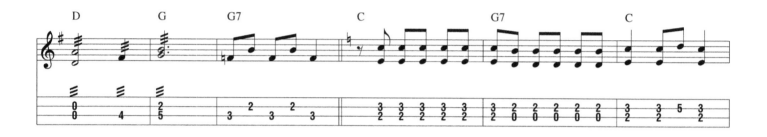

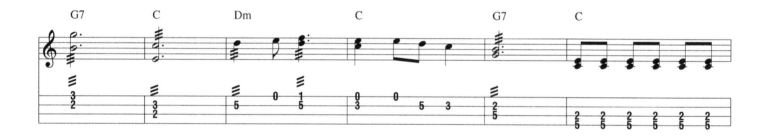

SUMMING UP — NOW YOU KNOW...

▶ *How to play a G major and C major scale*

▶ *How to use these scales to solo and play melodies in G and C*

▶ *How to add blue notes to the scales and play bluesy licks*

▶ *How to change any major scale to play in a minor key*

▶ *How to play double stops on G and C chords*

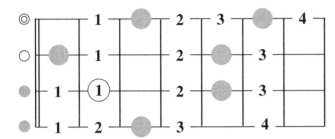 # FIRST POSITION MAJOR SCALES: E AND B

E Major Scale

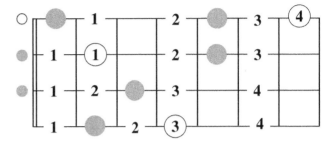

B Major Scale

WHY?

▶ These scales will help you play melodies and solos in the keys of E and B.

WHAT?

▶ *The root notes in each scale are circled.* The numbers are suggested fingerings.

▶ *The grey circles are "blue notes,"* flatted 3rds, 5ths and 7ths.

HOW?

▶ *Put your hand "in position" for each scale by fingering the appropriate chord.*

▶ *Play each scale until it feels comfortable and familiar.*

E Major Scale

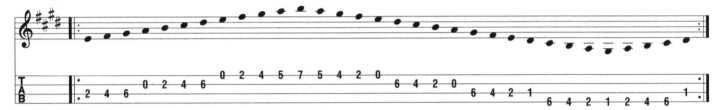

B Major Scale

DO IT!

▶ *Become familiar with the E and B major scales by playing these scale exercises:*

Descending E Scale Exercise

Descending B Scale Exercise

► The following folk-rock tune has a very popular chord progression used in countless songs. Throughout the chord changes, the mandolin ad libs E major scale licks. When the song modulates (changes keys) to B, the solo is based on the B major scale.

Rapid Eye Movement (In E and B)

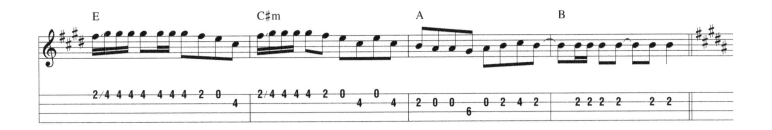

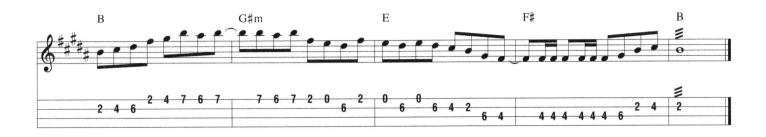

▶ The next tune, a twelve-bar blues, will prepare you to play honky-tonk, rock and roll or country tunes. There are plenty of blue notes mixed in with the E major scale in "Twelve Bar Stomp."

Twelve Bar Stomp

SUMMING UP — NOW YOU KNOW...

▶ *How to play an E major and B major scale*

▶ *How to use these scales to solo and play melodies in E and B*

▶ *How to add blue notes to the scales and play bluesy licks*

▶ *The meaning of the musical term "modulate"*

FIRST POSITION MAJOR SCALES: F AND B♭

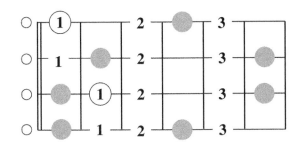 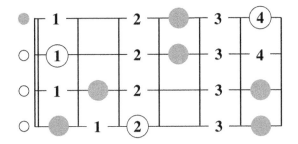

WHY?

▶ These scales will help you play melodies and solos in the keys of F and B♭.

WHAT?

▶ *The root notes in each scale are circled.* The numbers are suggested fingerings.

▶ *The grey circles are "blue notes,"* flatted 3rds, 5ths and 7ths.

HOW?

▶ *Put your hand "in position" for each scale by fingering the appropriate chord.*

▶ *Play each scale until it feels comfortable and familiar.*

F Major Scale

B♭ Major Scale

DO IT!

► *Become familiar with the F and Bb major scales by playing these scale exercises:*

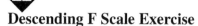

Descending F Scale Exercise

Ascending Bb Scale Exercise

► Here's a reprise of "Rapid Eye Movement," to illustrate the use of F and Bb major scales in this pop progression.

Rapid Eye Movement (In Bb and F)

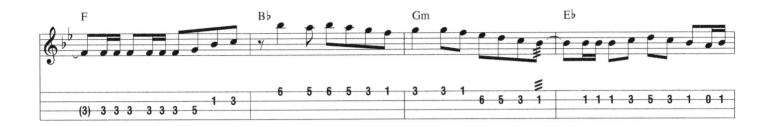

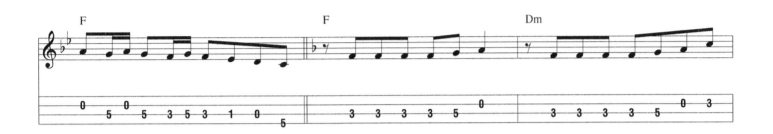

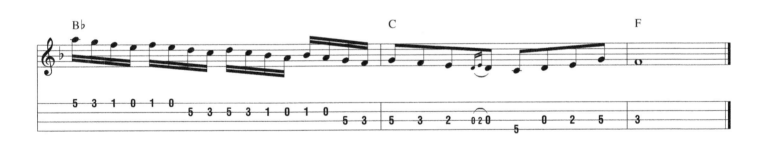

► This version of "Eight Bars and Eight Strings" features a bluesy solo in F and (after the tune modulates) in B♭. Popular blues standards that fit this eight-bar form include "How Long Blues," "When Things Go Wrong (It Hurts Me Too)," "You Got To Move" and "Sitting on Top of the World."

Eight Bars and Eight Strings (In F and B♭)

SUMMING UP — NOW YOU KNOW...

► *How to play F and B♭ major scales*

► *How to use these scales to solo and play melodies in F and B♭*

► *How to add blue notes to the scales and play bluesy licks*

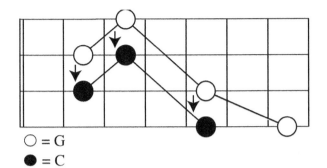

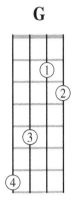

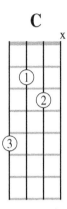

○ = G
● = C

WHY?

▶ It's called a "chop chord" because bluegrassers and anyone else who wants to play strong, rhythmic backup use this chord shape to play choppy, staccato chords on the second and fourth beats of each bar (the *backbeats*). This pushes the rhythm. Since this particular chord shape has no open strings, it can be damped after the chord is played for that percussive effect.

▶ Rhythm chops aside, the chop chords offer a system for playing moveable chords, scales and licks all over the fretboard.

WHAT?

▶ *The C chop chord is the same as the G chop chord "moved down a string,"* as **ROADMAP #7** illustrates.

▶ *Chop chords are "moveable" because they have no open* (unfretted) *strings.* Move a G chop chord up a fret and it becomes G♯.

▶ *The 1st and 3rd strings are the roots of the G chop chord.*

▶ *The 2nd and 4th strings are the roots of the C chop chord.*

HOW?

▶ *When you move the G-shaped chop chord "down a string" (e.g., from G to C, or A to D), you're going "up a 4th."* C is a 4th above G, D is a 4th above A.

● = G
○ = C

Moving the G chop chord "down a string" to go "up a fourth" to the C chop chord

▶ *When you move the C-shaped chop chord "up a string"* (from C to G, or D to A)*, you're going "up a 5th."*

▶ *To play chop chord rhythm, damp the strings with your fretting hand* immediately after stumming the chord. Strum brisk, strong downstrokes.

► *Learn the names of the chop chords all over the neck,* as shown below.

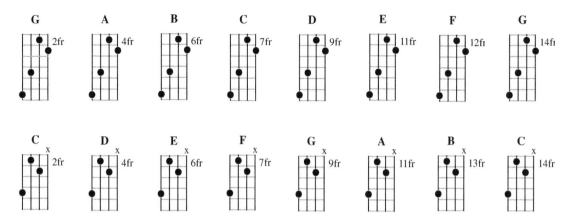

DO IT!

► "Wreck of Old 97," below, shows how to play typical bluegrass chop chord backup. The chops are played on the second and fourth beat of each bar.

Wreck of Old 97

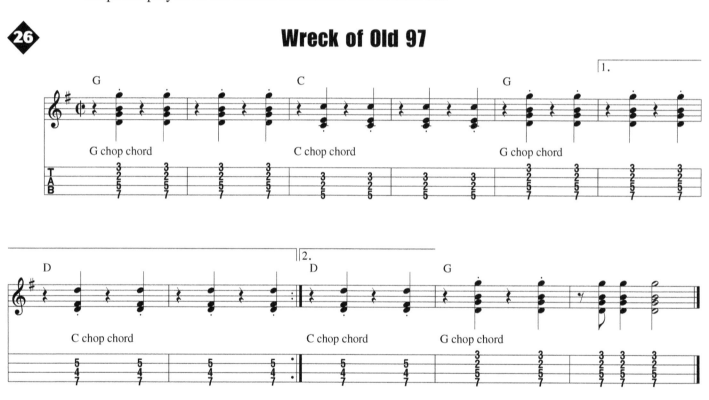

► *You can base countless licks and arpeggios on chop chords.* (To play an arpeggio, pick each of the notes of a chord separately, going up or down in pitch.) Most chop chord licks are "moveable"—many a G lick can be moved up the fretboard to become a G♯ lick, an A lick, and so on. The same lick can be played in C by "moving it down a string," then in D by moving the C lick up two frets, and so on.

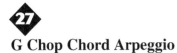

G Chop Chord Arpeggio   **The Same Arpeggio in A**   **G Chop Chord Arpeggio "Moved Down" to C**

► *The following bluegrass "tag endings" are moveable chop-chord licks.* A tag ending is used at the end of a verse or chorus, like a period at the end of a sentence.

"A" Tag Endings

The Same Tag Ending "Moved Down" to D

► The following solo to the old folk song, "The Sloop John B." consists of chop chord licks and arpeggios.

The Sloop John B.

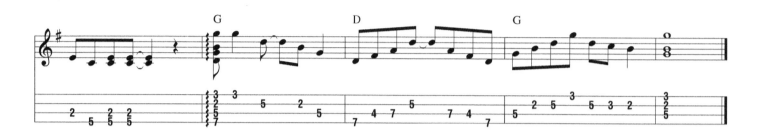

► *You can base many double stops on chop chords.*

G Chop Double-Stops

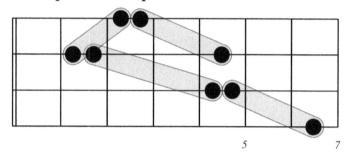

C Chop Double-Stops

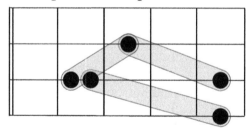

► The following solo for the old bluegrass standard, "Banks of the Ohio," consists of double stops derived from chop chords.

Banks of the Ohio

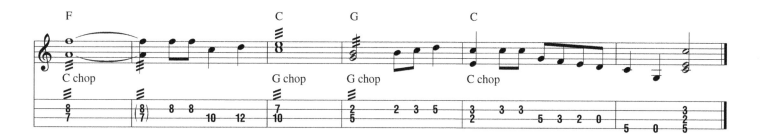

SUMMING UP — NOW YOU KNOW...

▶ *How to play chop chords all over the fretboard*

▶ *How to use them to play chop chord backup*

▶ *How to play moveable licks, arpeggios and solos based on chop chords*

▶ *How to play double stops based on chop chords*

▶ *The meaning of the musical term "arpeggio"*

#8 I–IV–V CHORD FAMILIES

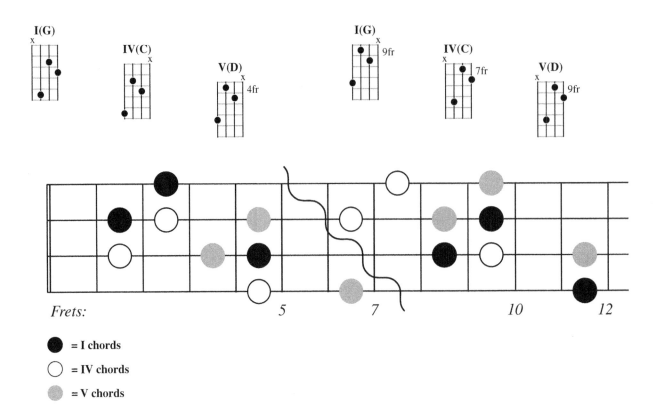

● = I chords

○ = IV chords

◐ = V chords

WHY?

▶ It's easier to learn new tunes and create solos when you understand "chord families" and know how to play them all over the fretboard. **ROADMAP #8** arranges the chop chords of **ROADMAP #7** into chord families (I, IV and V chords, described below). When you know how the IV chord and V chord sound, and you know where they are on the fretboard in relation to the I chord, you can make chord changes automatically, with a minimum of thought.

WHAT?

▶ *Every song has a chord progression,* a repeated chord sequence in which each chord is played for a certain number of bars.

▶ *Thousands of tunes consist of just three chords: the I, IV and V chord. These three chords are a "chord family."* "I," "IV" and "V" refer to the major scale intervals of the key.

▷ The I chord is the *key.* In the key of C, C is the I chord, because C is the first note in the C major scale.

▷ The IV chord is the chord whose root is the fourth note in the major scale of your key. In the key of C, F is the IV chord, since F is the fourth note in the C major scale.

▷ The V chord is the chord whose root is the fifth note in the major scale of your key. In the key of C, G is the V chord, since G is the fifth note in the C scale.

▶ **ROADMAP #8** *shows two ways of playing the "key of G" chord family:* with a G chop chord formation for a I chord, and with a C chop chord formation for a I chord.

▷ When the I chord is a G chop chord formation…

▼ *The IV chord is the C chop chord formation in the same place on the fretboard, down a string* (i.e., from strings 1, 2 and 3 to strings 2, 3 and 4).

Key of G

▼ *The V chord is the same chord formation as the IV chord, moved up two frets.*

Key of G

▷ *When the I chord is a C chop chord formation:*

▼ *The V chord is the G chop chord formation in the same place on the fretboard, up a string* (i.e., from strings 2, 3 and 4 to strings 1, 2 and 3).

Key of G

▼ *The IV chord is the same chord formation as the V chord, down two frets.*

Key of G

HOW?

▶ *The I–IV–V relationships are the same in all keys.* For example:

Key of A

   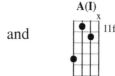

Key of D

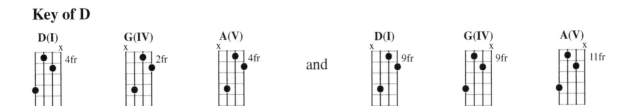

▶ ***Songs can be described (and understood) in I–IV–V terms.*** For example, the chord progression to "Great Speckled Bird," below, goes I, IV, V over and over, in that order. "Wreck of Old 97," which follows "Great Speckled Bird," has another popular I–IV–V progression: I–IV–I–V.

DO IT!

▶ ***Play chop chords to "Great Speckled Bird," to practice the I–IV–V configurations.*** It's an old gospel tune, and many other songs share the same melody and chord progression, including "I'm Thinking Tonight of My Blue Eyes," "Prisoner's Song" and "Wild Side of Life." This version starts in A, then modulates to D.

▶ ***Countless bluegrass standards have a I–IV–I–V*** progression similar to the following bluegrass standard, "Wreck of Old 97." The solo consists of arpeggios and tremolo chord licks in the key of A, using two different A chord families—one family has a C chop chord formation for the I chord, the other has a G chop chord formation for the I chord.

Wreck of Old 97 (With Chop Chord Licks)

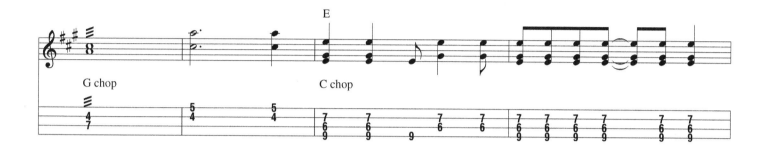

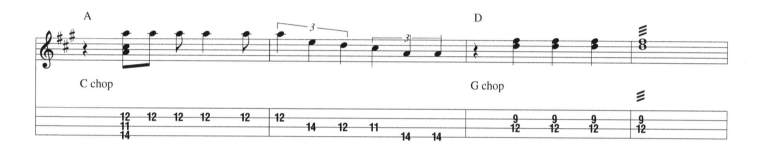

► *Many bluegrass, country, rock and folk standards are based on the twelve-bar blues progression:* "T for Texas," "I'm Movin' On," "Move It on Over," "Blue Suede Shoes," "Hound Dog," "Shake, Rattle and Roll," "Folsom Prison Blues," "Honky Tonk Blues" and "Muleskinner Blues" are a few examples. Here's a twelve-bar blues in A:

Key of A

Each of the twelve bars (measures) in the above blues progression has 4 beats. The repeat ∕ sign means play another bar of the chord in the previous bar.

During the twelve-bar blues in D that follows, the mandolin plays chop chords and other chord-based backup licks.

Blue Note Boogie

SUMMING UP — NOW YOU KNOW...

▶ *How to play two different chord families for any key*

▶ *How to use both chord families for backup and solos*

▶ *The meaning of these musical terms:*

I Chord, IV Chord, V Chord, Chord Family, Twelve-Bar Blues

#9 THE "K" POSITION

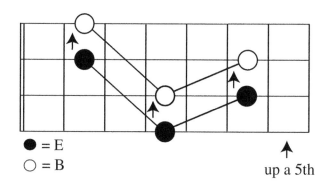

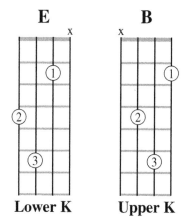

● = E
○ = B

up a 5th

Lower K   **Upper K**

Numbers indicate chord fingering

WHY?

▶ Many double stops, licks and scales can be derived from the K position. Like the chop chord, it's moveable and offers a frame of reference for playing all over the fretboard in all keys.

WHAT?

▶ *This three-finger chordal shape, which is not very useful as a chord, derives its name from its visual similarity to the letter K.*

upper K   **lower K**

▶ *It consists of two fifths, with a third in the middle:*

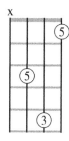   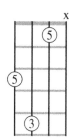

▶ *When you shift the K position up to higher strings (from 4–3–2 to 3–2–1), you move up a fifth.* **ROADMAP #9** illustrates this: the K position for the B chord is just "above" the E position, since B is a fifth above E.

► *Locate the lower K position* (*on strings 4-3-2*) *by relating it to the barred D formation, or to the "unplayed root"* on the 3rd string (same fret as the 2nd string):

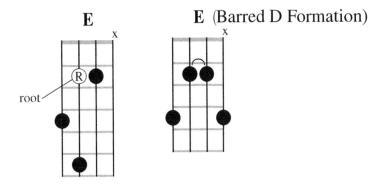

► *Locate the higher K position* (*on strings 3-2-1*) *by relating it to the "unplayed roots" on the 2nd and 4th strings* (as shown below) *or to the "barred G" chord position* indicated below, which has a 4th string root.

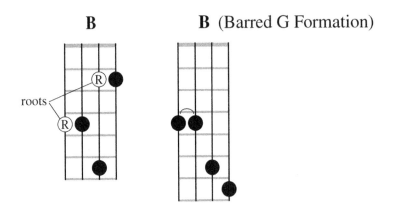

HOW?

► *The K position generates a series of double-stop harmonies.* Here are the lower K position double stops:

To play many of the above double stops, you have to move "off position." The numbers in the circles above indicate fingering for your chording hand.

Here are the double stops for the upper K position:

B

▶ *The K position is a frame of reference for major pentatonic scales and major scales.*
Here are the E major and E major pentatonic* scales, derived from the lower and upper
K positions:

E Major (from upper K position)

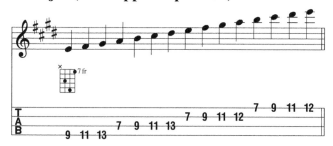

E Major Pentatonic (from upper K position)

E Major (from lower K position)

E Major Pentatonic (from lower K position)

* The *major pentatonic scale* is a five-note scale consisting of these intervals: I, II, III, V and VI.
  Hum the introductory riff to "My Girl" to hear it (the 6th note in the riff is a higher I).

DO IT!

► *The "I'm Okay, You're Okay Rag" consists of B, F# and E/K position scales and licks.*
It shows how easy it is to play in the key of B using K positions.

I'm Okay, You're Okay Rag

► *The following solo to the folk standard, "Banks of the Ohio," consists mostly of double stops of the E, A and B/K positions.*

Banks of the Ohio (With K Position Double Stops)

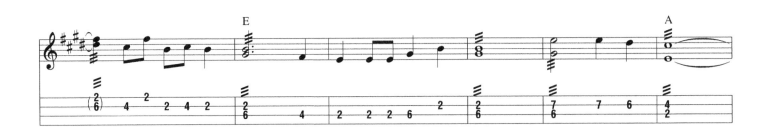

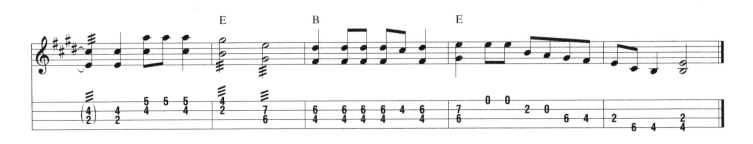

► *Many fiddle tunes are pentatonic.* Here's "Sally Goodin," played in the keys of F and C, using the pentatonic scales of the F and C/K positions.

Sally Goodin

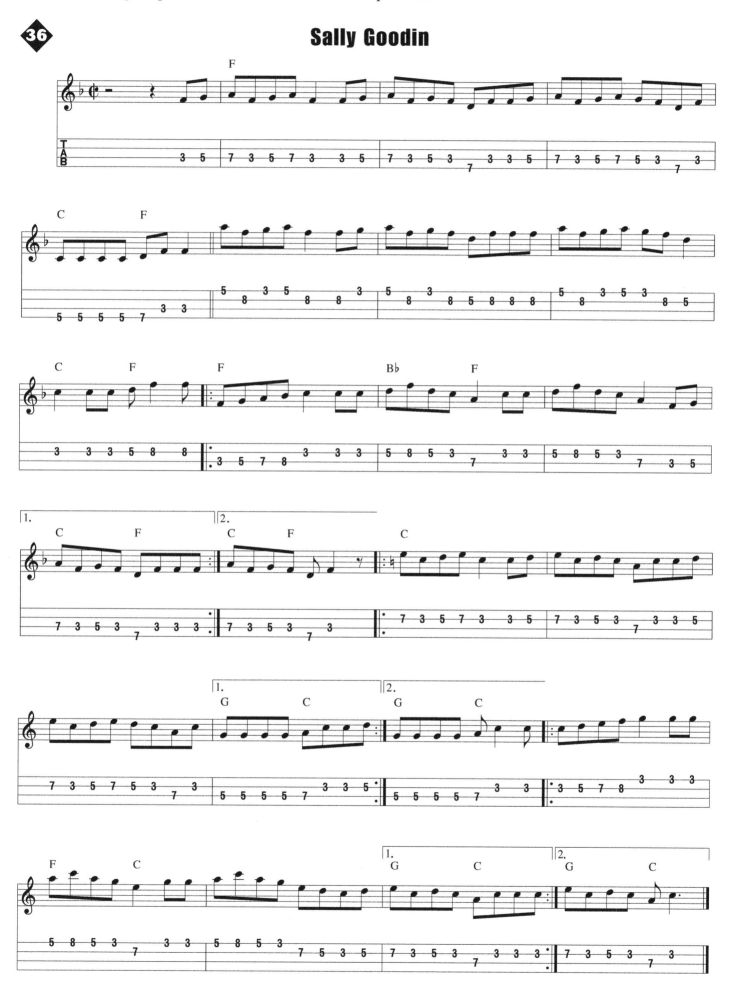

► *Countless tunes are built on the major scale of the I chord. The following version of "Red Wing," a folk song, shows how to play such a tune in the B♭/K position.*

Red Wing

► *You can adapt the K position to minor scales and double stops by flatting the thirds.* Here are the minor double stops of both K positions:

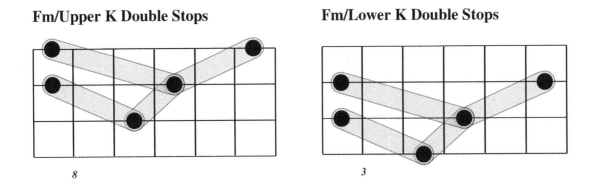

Fm/Upper K Double Stops

Fm/Lower K Double Stops

This solo for the gospel tune "Wayfaring Stranger," in the key of F minor, consists mostly of K position/minor double stops.

Wayfaring Stranger

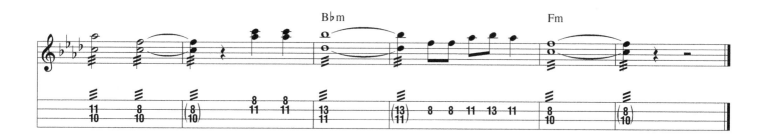

SUMMING UP — NOW YOU KNOW...

▶ *How to locate and play two K positions for any chord*

▶ *How to use the K positions to play double stops*

▶ *How to use the K positions to play major scales and major pentatonic scales*

▶ *How to use them to play minor double stops*

#10 ▸ COMBINING THE CHOP CHORD AND K SYSTEMS

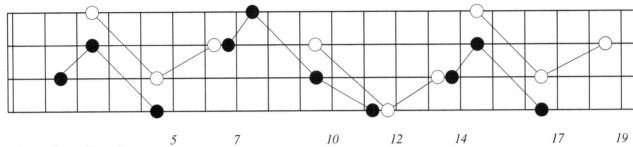

● = Chop Chords

○ = K Positions

WHY?

▶ By combining the chop chord and K systems, you can find multiple voicings of any chord. The resulting roadmap enables you to play melodies, chords and double stops all over the fretboard.

WHAT?

▶ **ROADMAP #10** *shows all the C chords and C/K positions.* To play ascending C chords, go from a chop chord to a K position; to a G chop chord formation, to a K position; to a C chop chord again (an octave higher) and so on, until you run out of frets.

▶ *Every chord has the same pattern.* For example, here are all the G chords and G/K positions:

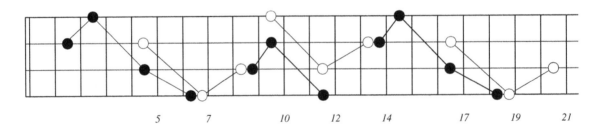

▶ *An ascending pattern of chop chords* is hidden in **ROADMAP #10** that can help you find all the chop chord formations for any chord. The two fretboard charts below illustrate the pattern:

C chop form—skip a fret—G chop form—skip a fret—C chop form—skip a fret and so on.

All the C Chords.

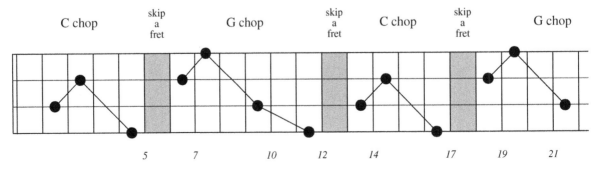

All the G Chords

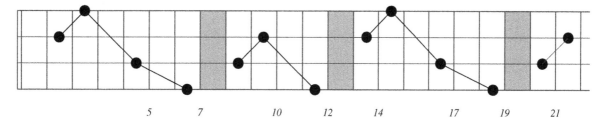

▶ *If you substitute the "barred D" chord formation for the lower (4th, 3rd and 2nd string) K position, you get this useful variation of* **ROADMAP #10:**

All the G Chords

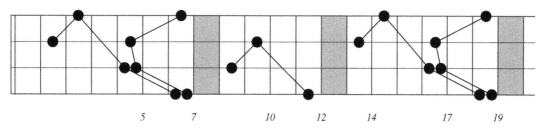

HOW?

▶ *Notice the linkage points as you play ascending formations of a chord.*

▷ *The K position of any chord starts at the 2nd fret of the C chop chord formation or the 4th fret of the G chop chord formation.:*

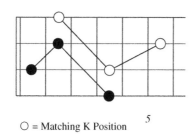

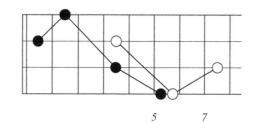

○ = Matching K Position

● = Chop Chord

▷ *A chop chord starts at the "high end" (the highest fret) of any K position:*

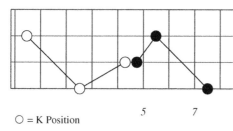

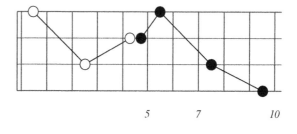

○ = K Position

● = Matching Chop Chord

47

DO IT!

▶ *Use* **ROADMAP #10** *to play ascending double stops for a chord.* For example, here are ascending double stops for a C chord:

 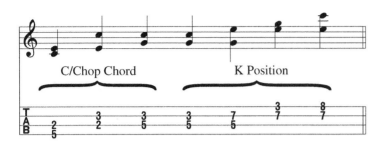

▶ Here are the same ascending double-stops for a G chord:

▶ *This arrangement of "Bury Me Beneath the Willow" uses D, G and A chop chords and K positions:*

Bury Me Beneath the Willow

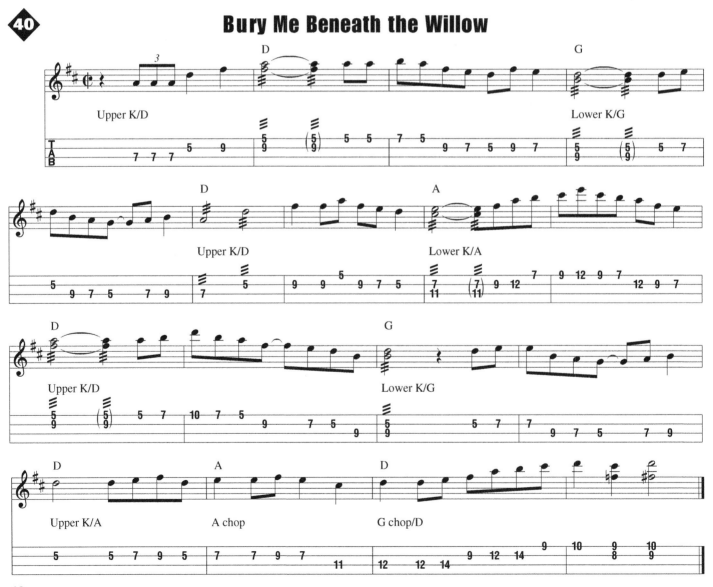

▶ *The following two tunes ("K Rations" and "Speckled Islands") have I–IV–V progressions, and both make use of K positions and chop chords.*

SUMMING UP — NOW YOU KNOW...

▶ *How to play any chord all over the fretboard using chop chords*

▶ *How to link the ascending chop chords to K positions, and vice versa*

▶ *How to play tunes with double stops, using both chop chords and K positions*

MOVEABLE CHORDS AND THEIR VARIATIONS

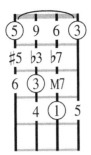 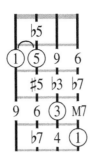 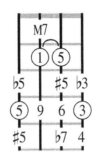 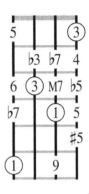

WHY?

▶ **ROADMAP #11** will help you build a full chord vocabulary. You'll find nearly every chord you need in this chapter, and some tips on how to remember them.

WHAT?

▶ *A chord is a group of three or more notes played simultaneously.*

▶ *A major chord consists of a root, 3rd and 5th.* That's why the four major chords of **ROADMAP #11** are made of circled 1s, 3s and 5s.

▶ *The other numbers in the grids above show the location of other intervals such as flatted 7ths, 9ths and flatted 3rds.*

▶ *You can play dozens of chords (minors, sevenths, major sevenths, etc.) by altering slightly the four moveable major chords of* **ROADMAP #11.** For example, you can play one fret lower on one string to make a major chord minor. This is an easy way to expand your chord vocabulary.

HOW?

▶ *There are four types of chords:*

▷ *Major chords* consist of a root (1), 3rd and 5th. Variations include:

▼ 6th: 1, 3, 5, 6

▼ Maj 7 (major 7): 1, 3, 5, 7

▼ + (augmented): 1, 3, ♯5

▷ *Minor chords* consist of a root, flatted 3rd and 5th. Variations include:

▼ m7 (minor 7): 1, ♭3, 5, ♭7

▼ m6: 1, ♭3, 5, 6

▼ m7♭5: 1, ♭3, ♭5, ♭7

▷ *Seventh chords* consist of a root, 3rd, 5th and flatted 7th. Variations:

▼ 9th: 1, 3, 5, ♭7, 9

▼ 7sus (suspended): 1, 4, 5, ♭7

▷ *Diminished chords* consist of a root, flatted 3rd, flatted 5th, and double-flatted 7th (which is the same as a 6th).

DO IT!

▶ *Play each basic major chord* (below) *and play its variations.* As you play each chord type (m7, Maj7, etc.), identify the intervals, e.g., "The second string is the 5th, the first string is the root," and so on.

▶ *Compare every new chord you learn to a basic chord you already know.* Every small chord grid in the "DO IT" section, below, is a variation of a basic chord formation.

▶ *Here are the most-played chords.* Play them and compare each formation to the larger grid to the left, from which it is derived.

"Barred G" Formation/A Chord

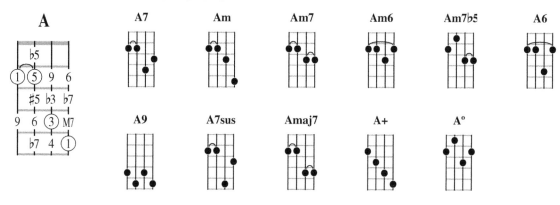

"Barred C" Formation/D Chord

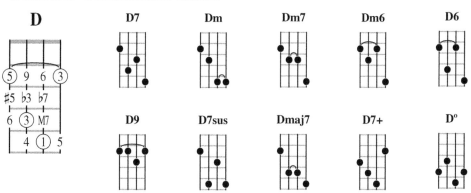

"Barred D" Formation/E Chord

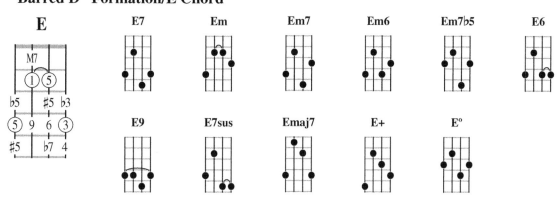

"C Chop Chord" Formation/D Chord

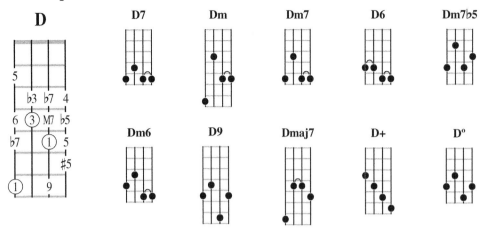

SUMMING UP — NOW YOU KNOW...

▶ *How to play any major chord four ways*

▶ *The formulas for major, 6th, augmented, major 7th, minor, minor 6th, minor 7th, minor 7th♭5, 7th, 9th, 7th suspended, and diminished chords*

▶ *How to vary four moveable major chords* to play the all these chords

#12 MOVEABLE MAJOR SCALES

"G Chop Chord" Formation

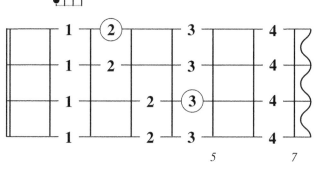

"Barred D Chord" Formation

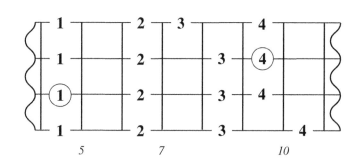

"C Chop Chord" Formation

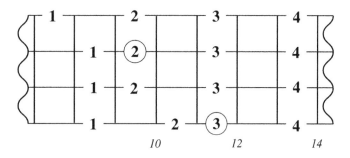

WHY?

▶ The major scale is the basis for countless melodies. Familiarity with moveable major scales allows you to play melodies and improvise solos. It brings you a step closer to any player's goal: to be able to *play* whatever you can hear.

WHAT?

▶ *Each of the three G major scales in* **ROADMAP #12** *is based on a moveable major chord.* The root notes are circled. Play the appropriate chord to get your fretting hand "in position" to play one of the major scales.

▶ *The numbers on* **ROADMAP #12** *are left-hand fingering suggestions.*

► **ROADMAP #12** *shows that there are three major scales for* <u>any</u> *chord.* **ROADMAP #9** shows you how to find any chord in several different places on the fretboard, using the same moveable chords that are shown in **ROADMAP #12.** Now you can play a major scale for three of those chord shapes. Here are the three key-of-C major scales, for example:

"C Chop Chord" Formation

"G Chop Chord" Formation

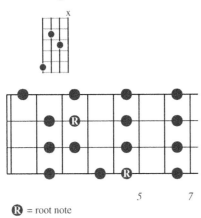

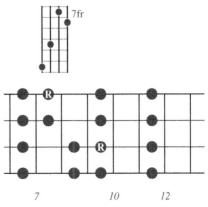

ℝ = root note

"Barred D Chord" Formation

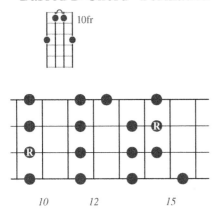

HOW?

► *Practice playing each moveable scale over and over until it comes naturally.* "Loop" them as shown below:

G Major Scale ("G Chop Chord")

G Major Scale ("Barred D")

G Major Scale ("C Chop Chord)

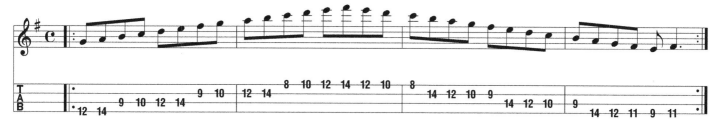

▶ *As long as a song stays in one key, you can ad lib solos based on the major scale of that key.*

DO IT!

▶ *Use D major scales to solo on "Two-for-Five," a country/rock ballad:*

Two-for-Five

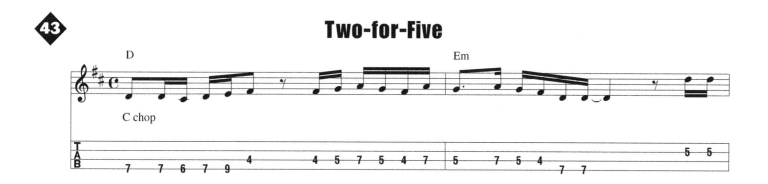

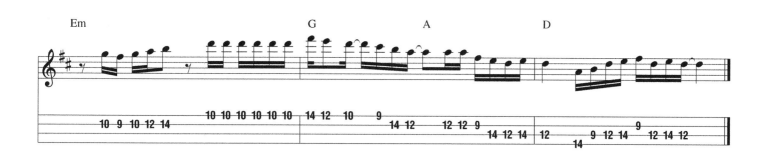

► *"Rural Highway" gives you a chance to practice soloing with moveable B♭ major scales:*

44 **Rural Highway**

► Here's yet another way to locate moveable major scales, based on the 'lead finger" — the finger that starts the scale. The following four D major scales each start with a different finger (the index, middle, ring or little finger) on a 4th string/D note. The resulting scales are useful and easy to locate.

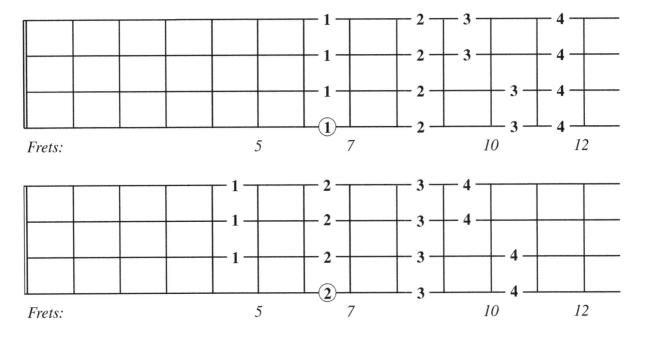

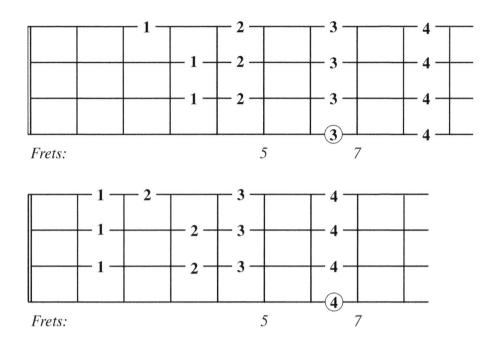

Frets: 5   7

Frets: 5   7

SUMMING UP — NOW YOU KNOW...

▶ *How to play three moveable major scales*

▶ *How to use them to ad lib solos or play melodies in any key*

▶ *Another set of four moveable major scales, each starting with a different finger on the 4th string/tonic (keynote)*

 **LISTENING SUGGESTIONS**

LISTENING SUGGESTIONS

Recordings are available by all these great mandolin players. Many of them also have videos, and most can be seen performing live—go see them!

BLUEGRASS

Bill Monroe, the father of bluegrass

Jesse McReynolds (of Jim and Jesse), pioneer of cross-picking

Sam Bush

Bob Applebaum
} these two players also play jazz
Andy Statman

Chris Thile

Tim O'Brien

Frank Wakefield

JAZZ AND WORLD MUSIC

Jethro Burns (of Homer and Jethro)

David Grisman

Dave Apollon

Don Stiernberg

Mike Marshall

Radim Zenkl

Paul Glasse

USING THE PRACTICE TRACKS

The **ROADMAPS** illuminate many soloing styles, including:

▶ *First position major scales*

▶ *First position major scales with double stops*

▶ *Chop chords and chop chord licks, arpeggios and tag endings*

▶ *Moveable major scales*

▶ *Moveable double stops based on the K position*

On the four practice tracks, the mandolin is separated from the rest of the band—it's on one side of your stereo. You can tune it out and use the band as backup, trying out any soloing techniques you like. You can also imitate the mandolin; here are the soloing ideas on each track:

Track #1: Circle of Fifths

Here's a chance to practice seven first position, major scales: E, A, D, G, C, F and B♭, in that order. The progression consists of four bars of each chord, with a country honky-tonk rhythm background. The mandolin plays double stops during the second time around the tune.

Track #2: Nine Pound Hammer (in E and A)

This simple bluegrass tune is played four times in E, then four times in A. In each key, the mandolin plays chop chord licks, arpeggios and tag endings during the first two passes, then plays first position major scale/licks with a heavy dose of blue notes the third and fourth times around. Here's the progression in both keys:

Key of E:

Key of A:

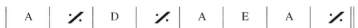

Track #3: Maggie May Not (in G)

The band plays this 16-bar rock progression three times, giving the mandolin a chance to exercise all three moveable major scales featured in **ROADMAP #12.** During the first 16 bars, the G chop chord/G major scale is used; the second time around, it's the barred D/G major scale; the third time, the mandolin plays the C chop chord/G major scale. Here's the progression:

Track #4: Chilly Winds (in D)

In this old folk tune, which is sometimes called "Lonesome Road Blues," the mandolin plays mostly double stops based on the D, G and A chop chords and K positions. The song has a country-rock feel, and this is the chord progression:

MANDOLIN NOTATION LEGEND

Legato Slide

Shift Slide

Tremolo

Hammer-On

Pull-Off

Hammer-On and Pull-Off

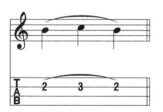

# ABOUT THE AUTHORS

FRED SOKOLOW is a versatile "musicians' musician." Besides fronting his own jazz, bluegrass and rock bands, Fred has toured with Bobbie Gentry, Jim Stafford, Tom Paxton, Ian Whitcomb, Jody Stecher and The Limeliters, playing guitar, banjo, mandolin and Dobro. His music has been heard on many TV shows (*Survivor, Dr. Quinn*), commercials and movies.

Sokolow has written nearly a hundred stringed instrument books and videos for seven major publishers. This library of instructional material, which teaches jazz, rock, bluegrass, country and blues guitar, banjo, Dobro and mandolin, is sold on six continents. He also teaches musical seminars on the west coast. A jazz CD, two rock guitar and two banjo recordings, which showcase Sokolow's technique, all received excellent reviews in the U.S. and Europe.

If you think Sokolow still isn't versatile enough, know that he MC'd for Carol Doda at San Francisco's legendary Condor Club, accompanied a Russian balalaika virtuoso at the swank Bonaventure Hotel in L.A., won the Gong show, played lap steel on the *Tonight Show*, picked Dobro with Chubby Checker, played mandolin with Rick James and wrote and performed the music score for the movie *Rampaging Nurses!*

BOB APPLEBAUM, mandolin virtuoso, has played with numerous acclaimed bluegrass groups since 1973. He has been a performing cast member of several TV shows and has performed and recorded mandolin music for theater, film and commercials. Widely recognized as the "teachers' teacher" of mandolin in Los Angeles, he has coached many well-known musicians on the finer points of mandolin playing. He developed and teaches the "K-position" method of understanding the mandolin fretboard that appears, for the first time in print, in this book.

Bob has recorded bluegrass and jazz mandolin albums, and his most recent offering, *All the Way Home,* has been widely hailed in bluegrass circles as "album of the year." He has been the subject of a *Scientific American* reader profile, and is co-creator of The Bluegrass Band virtual program for "Band in a Box."

Bob's thirty years of musical exploits include performances with a wide range of well-known players, from bluegrass legends like Mac Wiseman and Béla Fleck to jazzers like Sam Most. He coached Nicholas Cage for the film "Captain Corelli's Mandolin," and fronted the only band to tour the entire Alaskan Pipeline.

Learn to Play Today
with folk music instruction from Hal Leonard

Hal Leonard Bagpipe Method

The Hal Leonard Bagpipe Method is designed for anyone just learning to play the Great Highland bagpipes. This comprehensive and easy-to-use beginner's guide serves as an introduction to the bagpipe chanter. It includes access to online video lessons with demonstrations of all the examples in the book! Lessons include: the practice chanter, the Great Highland Bagpipe scale, bagpipe notation, proper technique, grace-noting, embellishments, playing and practice tips, traditional tunes, buying a bagpipe, and much more!

00102521 Book/Online Video $14.99

Hal Leonard Banjo Method – Second Edition

Authored by Mac Robertson, Robbie Clement & Will Schmid. This innovative method teaches 5-string, bluegrass style. The method consists of two instruction books and two cross-referenced supplement books that offer the beginner a carefully-paced and interest-keeping approach to the bluegrass style.

00699500 Book 1 Only...$9.99
00695101 Book 1 with Online Audio..............$17.99
00699502 Book 2 Only...$9.99
00696056 Book 2 with CD...............................$17.99

Hal Leonard Brazilian Guitar Method

by Carlos Arana

This book uses popular Brazilian songs to teach you the basics of the Brazilian guitar style and technique. Learn to play in the styles of Joao Gilberto, Luiz Bonfá, Baden Powell, Dino Sete Cordas, Joao Basco, and many others! Includes 33 demonstration tracks.

00697415 Book/Online Audio $17.99

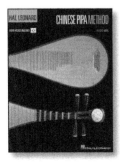

Hal Leonard Chinese Pipa Method

by Gao Hong

This easy-to-use book serves as an introduction to the Chinese pipa and its techniques. Lessons include: tuning • Western & Chinese notation basics • left and right hand techniques • positions • tremolo • bending • vibrato and overtones • classical pipa repertoire • popular Chinese folk tunes • and more!

00121398 Book/Online Video $19.99

Hal Leonard Dulcimer Method – Second Edition

by Neal Hellman

A beginning method for the Appalachian dulcimer with a unique new approach to solo melody and chord playing. Includes tuning, modes and many beautiful folk songs all demonstrated on the audio accompaniment. Music and tablature.

00699289 Book..$12.99
00697230 Book/Online Audio $19.99

Hal Leonard Flamenco Guitar Method

by Hugh Burns

Traditional Spanish flamenco song forms and classical pieces are used to teach you the basics of the style and technique in this book. Lessons cover: strumming, picking and percussive techniques • arpeggios • improvisation • fingernail tips • capos • and much more. Includes flamenco history and a glossary.

00697363 Book/Online Audio $17.99

Hal Leonard Irish Bouzouki Method

by Roger Landes

This comprehensive method focuses on teaching the basics of the instrument as well as accompaniment techniques for a variety of Irish song forms. It covers: playing position • tuning • picking & strumming patterns • learning the fretboard • accompaniment styles • double jigs, slip jigs & reels • drones • counterpoint • arpeggios • playing with a capo • traditional Irish songs • and more.

00696348 Book/Online Audio $12.99

Hal Leonard Mandolin Method – Second Edition

Noted mandolinist and teacher Rich Del Grosso has authored this excellent mandolin method that features great playable tunes in several styles (bluegrass, country, folk, blues) in standard music notation and tablature. The audio features play-along duets.

00699296 Book..$10.99
00695102 Book/Online Audio $16.99

Hal Leonard Oud Method

by John Bilezikjian

This book teaches the fundamentals of standard Western music notation in the context of oud playing. It also covers: types of ouds, tuning the oud, playing position, how to string the oud, scales, chords, arpeggios, tremolo technique, studies and exercises, songs and rhythms from Armenia and the Middle East, and 25 audio tracks for demonstration and play along.

00695836 Book/Online Audio $14.99

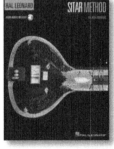

Hal Leonard Sitar Method

by Josh Feinberg

This beginner's guide serves as an introduction to sitar and its technique, as well as the practice, theory, and history of raga music. Lessons include: tuning • postures • right-and left-hand technique • Indian notation • raga forms; melodic patterns • bending strings • hammer-ons, pull-offs, and slides • changing strings • and more!

00696613 Book/Online Audio $16.99
00198245 Book/Online Media $19.99

Hal Leonard Ukulele Method

by Lil' Rev

This comprehensive and easy-to-use beginner's guide by acclaimed performer and uke master Lil' Rev includes many fun songs of different styles to learn and play. Includes: types of ukuleles, tuning, music reading, melody playing, chords, strumming, scales, tremolo, music notation and tablature, a variety of music styles, ukulele history and much more.

00695847 Book 1 Only...$7.99
00695832 Book 1 with Online Audio..............$12.99
00695948 Book 2 Only...$7.99
00695949 Book 2 with Online Audio..............$11.99

Hal Leonard Mandolin Play-Along Series

HAL•LEONARD® MANDOLIN PLAY-ALONG

AUDIO ACCESS INCLUDED

The Mandolin Play-Along Series will help you play your favorite songs quickly and easily. Just follow the written music, listen to the CD or online audio to hear how the mandolin should sound, and then play along using the separate backing tracks. Standard notation and tablature are both included in the book. The audio is enhanced so users can adjust the recording to any tempo without changing the pitch!

INCLUDES TAB

1. BLUEGRASS
Angeline the Baker • Billy in the Low Ground • Blackberry Blossom • Fisher's Hornpipe • Old Joe Clark • Salt Creek • Soldier's Joy • Whiskey Before Breakfast.
00702517 Book/Online Audio $14.99

2. CELTIC
A Fig for a Kiss • The Kesh Jig • Morrison's Jig • The Red Haired Boy • Rights of Man • Star of Munster • The Star of the County Down • Temperence Reel.
00702518 Book/Online Audio $14.99

3. POP HITS
Brown Eyed Girl • I Shot the Sheriff • In My Life • Mrs. Robinson • Stand by Me • Superstition • Tears in Heaven • You Can't Hurry Love.
00702519 Book/CD Pack................................$14.99

4. J.S. BACH
Bourree in E Minor • Invention No.1 (Bach) • Invention No.2 (Bach) • Jesu, Joy of Man's Desiring • March in D Major • Minuet in G • Musette in D Major • Sleepers, Awake (Wachet Auf).
00702520 Book/CD Pack................................$14.99

5. GYPSY SWING
After You've Gone • Avalon • China Boy • Dark Eyes • Indiana (Back Home Again in Indiana) • Limehouse Blues • The Sheik of Araby • Tiger Rag (Hold That Tiger).
00702521 Book/CD Pack................................$14.99

6. ROCK HITS
Back in the High Life Again • Copperhead Road • Going to California • Ho Hey • Iris • Losing My Religion • Maggie May • Sunny Came Home.
00119367 Book/Online Audio $16.99

7. ITALIAN CLASSICS
Come Back to Sorrento • La Spagnola • Mattinata • 'O Sole Mio • Oh Marie • Santa Lucia • Tarantella • Vieni Sul Mar.
00119368 Book/Online Audio $16.99

8. MANDOLIN FAVORITES
Arrivederci Roma (Goodbye to Rome) • The Godfather (Love Theme) • Misirlou • Never on Sunday • Over the Rainbow • Spanish Eyes • That's Amoré (That's Love) • Theme from "Zorba the Greek."
00119494 Book/Online Audio $14.99

9. CHRISTMAS CAROLS
Angels We Have Heard on High • Carol of the Bells • Go, Tell It on the Mountain • Hark! the Herald Angels Sing • Joy to the World • O Holy Night • Silent Night • We Wish You a Merry Christmas.
00119895 Book/CD Pack................................$14.99

10. SONGS FOR BEGINNERS
Amazing Grace • Cripple Creek • Devil's Dream • Frankie and Johnny • Frosty Morning • Over the Waterfall • Short'nin' Bread • Stone's Rag.
00156776 Book/Online Audio $14.99

11. CLASSICAL THEMES
Blue Danube Waltz • Eine Kleine Nachtmusik ("Serenade"), First Movement Excerpt • Für Elise • Humoresque • In the Hall of the Mountain King • La donna e mobile • The Merry Widow Waltz • Spring, First Movement.
00156777 Book/Online Audio $14.99

HAL•LEONARD®
www.halleonard.com

Prices, contents, and availability subject to change without notice.

Great Mandolin Songbooks
from Hal Leonard

THE BEATLES FOR SOLO MANDOLIN

20 favorite Beatles tunes in chord melody arrangements for mandolin including: All You Need Is Love • Blackbird • Can't Buy Me Love • Eight Days a Week • Here Comes the Sun • Hey Jude • In My Life • Let It Be • Michelle • Strawberry Fields Forever • Twist and Shout • We Can Work It Out • Yesterday • and more.
00128672...$16.99

CHRISTMAS CAROLS FOR MANDOLIN

23 Christmas songs arranged especially for mandolin, including: Away in a Manger • The First Noel • God Rest Ye Merry, Gentlemen • Hark! the Herald Angels Sing • It Came upon the Midnight Clear • Jingle Bells • O Christmas Tree • O Holy Night • Silent Night • Up on the Housetop • We Wish You a Merry Christmas • What Child Is This? • and more.
00699800...$10.99

CLASSICAL SOLOS FOR MANDOLIN

This publication contains 20 classical mandolin pieces compiled, edited, and performed by world-renowned virtuoso Carlos Aonzo. The music is arranged in order of difficulty beginning with exercises by Giuseppe Branzoli and finishing with complete concert pieces using the most advanced mandolin techniques. Pieces include: Andante – Pizzicato on the Left Hand (Carlo Munier) • Exercise in A Major (Giuseppe Branzoli) • La Fustemberg (Antonio Riggeiri) • Partita V in G minor Overture (Filippo Sauli) • Theme with Variations in A Major (Bartolomeo Bortolazzi) • and more.
00124955 Book/Online Audio.........................$19.99

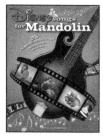

DISNEY SONGS FOR MANDOLIN

25 classic melodies from Disney's finest productions over the years presented in arrangements for mandolin. Includes: The Bare Necessities • Be Our Guest • Circle of Life • Colors of the Wind • Go the Distance • Heigh-Ho • It's a Small World • Mickey Mouse March • A Spoonful of Sugar • Under the Sea • When You Wish upon a Star • Zip-A-Dee-Doo-Dah • and more.
00701904...$12.99

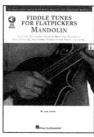

FIDDLE TUNES FOR FLATPICKERS: MANDOLIN

Now you can learn to play famous fiddle tunes specially arranged for mandolin. Get started flatpickin' now with songs like: Blackberry Blossom • Kentucky Mandolin • Old Joe Clark • Salt Creek • Turkey in the Straw • and more. The accompanying audio features specially mixed tracks that let you hear the mandolin alone, the mandolin with the backing track, or just the backing track so you can play along!
14011276 Book/Online Audio.........................$17.99

FIRST 50 SONGS YOU SHOULD PLAY ON MANDOLIN

A fantastic collection of 50 accessible, must-know favorites for the beginner who's learned enough to start playing popular songs: Amazing Grace • Crazy • Cripple Creek • Folsom Prison Blues • Friend of the Devil • Hallelujah • Ho Hey • I Am a Man of Constant Sorrow • I Walk the Line • I'll Fly Away • Losing My Religion • Maggie May • Mr. Bojangles • Rocky Top • Take Me Home, Country Roads • Tennessee Waltz • Wagon Wheel • Wildwood Flower • Yesterday • and more.
00155489 Tab, Chords & Lyrics.....................$15.99

FOLK SONGS FOR MANDOLIN

SING, STRUM & PICK ALONG
More than 40 traditional favorites arranged specifically for mandolin: Arkansas Traveler • Buffalo Gals • (I Wish I Was In) Dixie • Home on the Range • I've Been Working on the Railroad • Man of Constant Sorrow • Michael Row the Boat Ashore • My Old Kentucky Home • Oh! Susanna • She'll Be Comin' 'Round the Mountain • Turkey in the Straw • The Wabash Cannon Ball • When the Saints Go Marching In • Yankee Doodle • and more!
00701918...$16.99

THE HAL LEONARD MANDOLIN FAKE BOOK

This collection packs 300 songs into one handy songbook: As Time Goes By • Bad, Bad Leroy Brown • Can't Take My Eyes off of You • Daydream Believer • Edelweiss • Fields of Gold • Going to California • Hey, Soul Sister • Ho Hey • I'm Yours • Island in the Sun • King of the Road • Losing My Religion • Maggie May • Over the Rainbow • Peaceful Easy Feeling • Redemption Song • Shenandoah • Toes • Unchained Melody • Wildwood Flower • You Are My Sunshine • and many more.
00141053 Melody, Lyrics & Chords $39.99

MASTERS OF THE MANDOLIN

This collection of 130 mandolin solos is an invaluable resource for fans of bluegrass music. Each song excerpt has been meticulously transcribed note-for-note in tab from its original recording so you can study and learn these masterful solos by some of the instrument's finest pickers. From the legendary Bill Monroe to more contemporary heroes like Sam Bush and Chris Thile, and even including some non-bluegrass greats like Dave Apollon and Jethro Burns, this book contains a wide variety of music and playing styles to enjoy.
00195621...$24.99

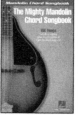

THE MIGHTY MANDOLIN CHORD SONGBOOK

Lyrics, chord symbols, and mandolin chord diagrams for 100 pop and rock hits: Blowin' in the Wind • Crazy Little Thing Called Love • Dance with Me • Edelweiss • Georgia on My Mind • Hey Jude • I Feel the Earth Move • Jolene • Lean on Me • Me and Bobby McGee • Mean • No Woman No Cry • Patience • Ring of Fire • Sweet Caroline • This Land Is Your Land • Unchained Melody • Wonderwall • and many more.
00123221...$17.99

O BROTHER, WHERE ART THOU?

This collection contains both note-for-note transcribed mandolin solos, as well as mandolin arrangements of the melody lines for 11 songs: Angel Band • The Big Rock Candy Mountain • Down to the River to Pray • I Am a Man of Constant Sorrow • I Am Weary (Let Me Rest) • I'll Fly Away • In the Highways (I'll Be Somewhere Working for My Lord) • In the Jailhouse Now • Indian War Whoop • Keep on the Sunny Side • You Are My Sunshine.
00695762 Tab, Chords & Lyrics.....................$15.99

THE ULTIMATE MANDOLIN SONGBOOK

arr. Janet Davis
The Ultimate Mandolin Songbook contains multiple versions varying in difficulty of 26 of the most popular songs from bluegrass, jazz, ragtime, rock, pop, gospel, swing and other genres, in both standard notation and mandolin tab. Songs: Alabama Jubilee • Autumn Leaves • The Entertainer • Great Balls of Fire • How Great Thou Art • Limehouse Blues • Orange Blossom Special • Rawhide • Stardust • Tennessee Waltz • Yesterday • You Are My Sunshine • and more!
00699913 Book/Online Audio.......................$34.99